The Universe Speaks: Talks To Empower You

SEPTEMBER 28, 2019

ANNAPOLIS, MD

TABLE OF CONTENTS

SCHEDULE OF EVENTS

9:30-10:00am   Lobby:
Registration

10:00-10:15am   Main Stage:
Welcome

10:15-11:15am   Main Stage: Sev
Powerful Manifestation

11:30am-12:30pm   Main Stage: Randi
Understanding the Human Energy Grid

12:45 - 1:45pm   Dining Room:
Catered lunch

2:00-3:00pm   Main Stage: Sev
Your Psychic Abilities in a Quantum World

3:15-4:15pm   Main Stage: Sev
Ask Sev

4:30-6:00pm   Lounge
Book Signing & Social Time with Sev & Randi

WELCOME

We are honored to spend the day with you today at *The Universe Speaks: Talks To Empower You.* We hope today's messages expand your awareness, creating an energetic pathway through our Quantum World to allow the expression of your authenticity, for your true self is a gift to Earth and all beings dwelling on it.

Evolve through Love,

Sev and Randi

SEV TOK

Sev is originally from Istanbul, Turkey having emigrated to the Washington DC suburbs as a little girl. The first few years living in America, she did not know English and relied on her intuition to understand the people and situations surrounding her. This began her focus on accessing inter-dimensional information.

After earning a Bachelor of Science degree in Biology from Loyola University in Baltimore, Sev began her adult journey of suppressing her true self. She hid her para-normal abilities and kept quiet a huge secret: her life-long ET Contact. Through decades of self-induced struggles, difficult relationships, and efforts to mask her authenticity, Sev finally allowed herself to express her true identity. Ten years ago, she became a Spiritual Counselor conducting Soul Sessions and quit her office job to conduct her intuitive readings full time.

Sev wasn't finished though. She still had one more hurdle to plow through on her journey of authenticity. After coming face-to-face with Greys in September 2017 on the Inner Banks of North Carolina, where Sev currently resides, she experienced a dramatic mind shift. The Greys marked her body with two red X-marks prompting her to finally face her biggest fear yet: the reality of her ET Contact. In August 2018, Sev wrote her "coming out" book, *You Have The Right To Talk To Aliens.*

Her book opened many doors including an invitation from AlienCon (a division of the TV show *Ancient Aliens*) to be a Guest Speaker in Baltimore, November 2018. Since then, Sev has been interviewed by radio shows around the world and continues to work with Experiencers, helping them process and understand their remarkable ET Contact.

Sev created *The Universe Speaks: Talks To Empower You* to provide a platform for those working in the field of Quantum Consciousness and ET Research to speak and share their knowledge. One cannot talk about our Quantum Reality without discussing other dimensions which hold infinite forms of life.

Sev gives a special thank you to *Cecilia Benalcazar*, who is not only a long-time friend but a supporter and cheerleader, whose expertise and guidance as the Event Coordinator for today's event has made it possible for us to share in this day together.

Sev offers **Soul Sessions** in person and through Zoom, FaceTime, and Skype.

Soul Sessions provide channeled information focused on igniting your authentic self so that you can be the best version of yourself. Sev can hear, feel, and see inter-dimensional information from your Spirit Guides, personal energy, and from the matrix of information floating around us in the multi-dimensions. Everyone can access the same information that Sev does. All it takes is focus and practice.

There are a variety of *Soul Sessions* available: *What's My Soul Purpose, Unleash My Potential, Tweak My Energy to Manifest, Past Lives, Making Contact, Fulfilling Career, Better Relationships, Elevate.* For information on each *Soul Session*, please visit planetsev.com

Sev also offers help for Experiencers through her free forum, **ET Encounters**, on her website. If you have had ET Contact and need help understanding and processing your incredible experience, please take advantage of this free forum. Sev respects and honors your privacy. Portions of some ET Stories are shared, anonymously, on **True ET Stories** on Sev's website. Reading Experiencer's stories can help those grappling with their own Encounters. ET Contact is a genuine experience experienced by millions world-wide.

Sev's newly created **Alien Spirit TV** on youtube has videos about her ET Contact, Interviews, the 10-part series *How to Activate Your Ascension All By Yourself,* Spiritual Information, *Stranger Things: A Review of the Paranormal* about how the hit TV show, and much more.

Sev is available for interviews, panel discussions, consultations, talks, workshops, and writing projects. Please contact Sev at sev@planetsev.com

For more information about Sev and her offerings:

Email: sev@planetsev.com

Website: planetsev.com

      ET Encounters

      True ET Stories

      Soul Sessions

      Newsletter

      Videos

      Events

      Radio/Youtube Interviews

Youtube: Alien Spirit TV with Sev

Facebook, Instagram, Twitter: Sev Tok

Facebook: The Universe Speaks

You Have The Right To Talk To Aliens: Amazon

RANDI BOTNICK

Randi began her healing career in the late 1990s after receiving her training as a Sekhem-Seichim-Reiki Master Teacher. Since then, she has studied various mind-body practices including yoga therapy, Clinical Hypnotherapy and the Results System®. She has a thriving spiritual counseling and energy healing practice, both in-person and online.

In the spring of 2010, while meditating, Randi spontaneously began channeling the Ashtar Command, a group of Lightbeings and angels who are assisting us as the Earth and all of her inhabitants move into the fourth dimension.

In 2014, the Federation of Councils introduced themselves to Randi as a benevolent group of Lightbeings here to support us at this time. They are at the core of her spiritual healing team, offering her clients information and relief in all aspects of their lives.

Randi offers both **Spiritual Counseling** and **Energy Healing** sessions. *Spiritual Counseling* includes discussing symptoms and challenges and working through how experiences and belief systems that originated in the past are causing life to unfold as it is. Helping people understand their place in the world and how they contribute to creating their own life experiences, while honoring their spiritual belief system, is a core part of this therapy. Every issue in our lives has a spiritual component. Do we believe in a higher power? Do we believe we are loved unconditionally by the Universe? Do we trust in Universal nourishment and support?

Energy Healing takes place multi-dimensionally, and The Federation of Councils, our guides, the Archangels, Masters and Teachers join us in the healing space. While working in the etheric field, they provide healing on the four bodies — physical, mental, emotional and spiritual — and delete pain and suffering from karma, genetic lineages and ancestry. The team provides personal information and guidance for future change.

Randi sees private patients, conducts distant healings for groups or individuals, and teaches classes and workshops. Please contact Randi at randi@randibotnick.com.

For more information about Randi and her offerings:

Phone: 443.621.6059

Email: randi@randibotnick.com

Website: randibotnick.com

      Sessions

      Events

      Classes

      Store

      Blog

4th Dimensional Healing: A New Paradigm For Healing:
Amazon and 4dhealingguide.com

ALIEN NEIGHBORHOOD
from Sev's book,
You Have The Right To Talk To Aliens

I used to be a card-carrying alien. I traded in my green-colored alien card for a piece of paper declaring my American citizenship in 1995. According to the IRS, an alien is someone who is not a U.S. national or U.S. citizen. I am not an alien anymore, under the laws of the U.S. government. However, when I visit another country, I am an alien to that country. I am also an alien to any being not from Earth. We are all aliens in the eyes of someone.

If you believe Earthlings are the only intelligent beings in all the galaxies, you are in for an awakening for two reasons. First, we are not all that intelligent. If you insist we are, then why can't we explain gravity, how bees fly, what dreams are, how the Great Pyramid of Giza was built, and why dogs prefer to poop facing north or south?

Second, mathematic probability supports that we are not alone. Scientists estimate there are ten trillion galaxies in the universe. Using data from the Kepler telescope, there are an estimated nineteen sextillion stars similar to our Sun with a planet similar to Earth.[1] What are the odds that humans are the only advanced species in the galaxy? One in 60 bil-

---

[1] Forbes.com, Nov. 2017, The Number of Earth-Like Planets in the Universe is Staggering - Here's the Math.

lion.[2] There is a better chance you will get hit by lightning, eaten by a shark, date a supermodel, win the Powerball, or achieve sainthood than the chance that humans are the only advanced lifeforms in the universe.[3]

We may not be the most intelligent beings, but we are intelligent enough to desire more intelligence. And that is where the aliens come into play. Imagine what life on Earth could be like if we freely engaged in communication with beings from other planets. What would they teach us? If we formed alliances with other intelligent life we could learn to create a world where there is free energy, no war, no hunger, no killing, teleportation, a cleaner planet, and a healthier population.

Maybe you think alien life will destroy us. If they were out to burn us to bits, it would have happened already. It is not aliens who pose the fear of wiping out humanity, it is humans. We are a mean bunch. We like to kill. We like to take over. We like to steal and we like to control.

What intelligent alien would intentionally land here to risk death due to our ignorance and hostile attitude? For those of you who ask why a spaceship doesn't land in front of the White House, there is your answer. Don't for one

---

[2]Airspacemag.com, May 2016, The Odds That We're the Only Advanced Species in the Galaxy are One in 60 Billion.

[3] bostonglobe.com, August 2017, These Extremely Rare Things are More Likely to Happen to You Than Winning the Powerball Jackpot.

minute think that a spaceship landing on the North Lawn would create a peaceful incident. It would be chaotic and with our quick trigger fingers, there would be death.

Our political, social, and cultural frameworks will probably be shaken if we gain knowledge from an advanced civilization. This is often what change does. It shakes things up. It causes distress. Some will lose fortunes, some will gain fortunes. For the ones who have a tight grip on our economic and political institutions, a change towards a kinder, gentler Earth could cause them to lose what they hold so dear: power and money.

We are not ready for an alien landing. We need to purge and heal many of our societal ills first. I believe we are in the process of that. The current political climate in the U.S. is illuminating the serious problems in our governmental institutions. We also haven't learned to love one another. We are still working on that. Until we accept and love one another, how can we harmoniously interact with an alien civilization? We need to make peace at home first, before extending peace to another civilization. Otherwise, we will inflict upon them the fears and hostilities we inflict upon one another here on Earth.

Right now, we live like the kid whose mom won't let him play with the neighbors. We have chosen to isolate ourselves from the rest of the cosmos. All the reasons for hiding and covering up the truth, I do not know. What I do know is that we are in a reveal. The truth is being divulged in a variety of ways through books and movies and TV shows. There is a momentum gaining intensity and soon, Earthlings will have to acknowledge they share the universe with other intelligent life.

Our lack of planetary peace does not stop aliens or ETs from visiting us. ET stands for extraterrestrial. The Merriam-Webster definition of extraterrestrial is *"originating, existing, or occurring outside the earth or its atmosphere."* Currently, there are two schools of thought regarding ET contact. One is the extraterrestrial hypothesis (ETH) and the other is the inter-dimensional hypothesis (IDH). Both are attempts to make sense of something which we fully do not understand.

The origins of ETH and IDH are unknown. There have been several scientists, astronomers, and UFOologists referring to these hypotheses for decades.

ETH is based on the belief that ETs are living beings, visiting from another planet. They get into a flying saucer, zip through space, and enter our atmosphere. They walk around and sometimes interact with humans. Sometimes, they don't leave their spaceships but fly around for us to see them. They have technology more advanced than ours, explaining how they zip through space. If we could move through space as quickly as they, we would be able to visit their planets and interact with them too. All of this is predicated on the belief that we and the ETs live in the same dimension.

IDH is based on the belief that ETs are living beings, visiting from other dimensions. They get into a flying saucer, zip through dimensions and enter our reality but not our three dimensional reality. The ETs communicate with us in the dimensions beyond the three we know of. There are more than three dimensions on Earth. According to quantum physics, there are many dimensions and many universes, or multiverses.

A dimension is a level of reality. Humans see in three dimensions, or 3D. The first dimension gives us length, such as a straight line drawn on paper. The second dimension adds height, such as a square drawn on paper. The third dimension adds depth, such as a cube. The Superstring Theory, in quantum physics, postulates there are ten dimensions in the universe. The fourth dimension is time, the fifth dimension is a band from the sixties or where parallel worlds exist, the sixth through tenth dimensions are also planes of reality where other worlds or multiverses exist. I personally believe there are more than ten dimensions. I believe there are an infinite number of dimensions.

You are more than 3D. You exist in multiple dimensions beyond three. Don't believe me? Then point to your mind. You can't. You can point to your brain, but you cannot point to your mind. There is no anatomy book which locates the mind. Point to your soul. You can't. Point to your higher self. You can't. Your mind, soul, and higher self exist in dimensions beyond the first, second, and third. Your 3D self is just a sliver of your whole self.

You cannot see many dimensions because they are composed of energy having frequencies higher than what your eyes can register. This is why you cannot see your mind, soul, and higher self. Just because you can't see them doesn't mean they don't exist. You can't see microwaves, radio waves, and sound waves, but you know they exist.

There is an energy field, or aura, surrounding you. Everything exudes energy, this is scientifically proven. This energy field emits color and sound. You are actually a walking orchestra and light show. You can see the auras of humans and animals. It just takes practice. Your eyes can be trained to see some of the higher frequencies.

The part of you existing in the higher dimensions communicates with beings in the higher dimensions. You have the 3D part of you communicating with 3D beings and you have the '3D plus' parts of you communicating with a different set of beings

Every day, billions of people around the world have inter- dimensional communication with a being living in another dimension. It is called a prayer. There are different types of prayers. One type is a conversation with a non-human entity such an angel or spirit guide. You cannot see the entity because it does not live on Earth. This being knows everything about you. You believe it can manipulate events to make your prayers come true. This being is all knowing, having more knowledge about the universe than you do. And you trust it whole heartedly. You put your life in its hands. Does this make logical sense? No! Is this type of inter-dimensional communication socially acceptable? Yes!

By definition, any being which does not reside on Earth is an extraterrestrial or ET. Wouldn't that include angels, spirit guides, Hindu gods, and others? If Jesus lives in Heaven, which exists outside of Earth's atmosphere, and you believe him to be a living being, that makes him an ET.

Why does our Western society say it's ok to talk to some otherworldly beings but not to others? If I told a stranger on the street that I had a conversation with an angel this morning, they would not blink twice. If I told the same stranger I talked to an ET this morning, they would think I am crazy. When we stop picking and choosing which ETs are socially acceptable to talk to and which ones aren't, we will end the hypocrisy. And don't forget you, too, are an ET in the eyes of other inter-stellar beings.

Since Earthlings are violent, visiting ETs are safer using the IDH method of interaction. Many people are having ET contact via this method whether they know it or not. Inter-dimensional ET contact is often misinterpreted as dreams or hallucinations, if you even remember them. Most

inter-dimensional ET contact is not consciously remem-
bered. The 3D portion of your brain can't compute the multi-
dimensional, so it does one of two things. One, the brain may
place the event in the subconscious. This is why some experiencers (the term abductee is no longer used) undergo hypno-
sis. Two, the brain may search for a logical explanation, iden-
tify-ing the event as a dream or hallucination. Logical expla-
nations are not always correct.

Hence, the dilemma of inter-dimensional experiencers: we think we are crazy or making things up. The higher self knows what happened was not a dream. Our gut tells
us it was not imaginary. We have a deep knowing that the
dream is real. However, we cannot logically explain it to
ourselves and to others. So, we try to dismiss it. We try to file
it away, but the truth cannot be buried. As long as we are
stuck on explaining every-thing in terms of a three dimensional framework, we are not going to understand how ET
contact and the universe work.

There are ETs similar to us frequency-wise but are
much more advanced. Maybe these ETs are us in the future.
It is quite possible that our future selves can go back and
forth between the past and the future. There are many kinds
of advanced ETs and maybe our future selves are just one
type.

The most popular type of ET, due to movies, TV, and
books, is the Grey. It is the kind of ET with a big head and

large dark eyes, with a tiny nose and mouth. It has two arms and two legs and is much smaller than us in stature. They don't speak aloud with words. They speak telepathically.

The Greys are not the only type of ET. There are documented reports of ETs who look similar to us but taller, some that look like giant bugs, and some who look like a cross between a reptile and a human. How many types of ETs are there? Unlimited amounts. If we try to calculate all the planets and stars in the universe multiplied by all the dimensions, that equates to limitless amounts of possible life forms.

There is a slow reveal going on. Our governments are coming out with the truth about our ET relationships. It is happening in dosages we can handle. The more we, the people, demand a higher dosage, the more we will be given what we need. It all depends on how much we push the leaders of our countries for the truth. We, the people, outnumber all the Presidents, Prime Ministers, billionaires, industry leaders, and media moguls, yet we allow them to determine what universal truths we know and when we know it.

This book is my personal effort to join the global momentum towards truth. I have embarked on the journey of personal authenticity and, lo and behold, ETs came up. I didn't know that was going to happen when I started my path of spiritual awakening. The ET truth was presented to me in a way which I cannot ignore nor completely understand. It freaked me out and confused the hell out of me. The hardest part was hiding it. I tried for many years to ignore my experiences, but what happened to me the second night I moved to Arapahoe, North Carolina, made it impossible for me to keep quiet.

Why am I on this difficult journey of authenticity and spiritual awakening? Because I desire personal peace. I desire it more than anything. My desire for peace makes me look in the dark corners of my mind and shine light on what I have been hiding. The reveal isn't pretty. Identifying the protective layers, or lies, I piled on to shield me from the truth is imperative. I must shed these layers or I cannot fulfill my potential and create a life of fulfillment. What is my potential and the potential of every human? A life of internal peace.

In my quest to fulfill my potential, I cannot smother the authentic version of myself. I yearn to live on a planet which also displays its authentic version of itself. Just as I peel back the lies about myself, I want our society to peel back its lies about itself. I believe denying the truth about who we are prevents us from finding peace, personally and collectively.

In this book, I present a very fast history of my life as it applies to the struggles of accepting my ET contacts. I share with you some of my supernatural incidents to illustrate the fact that we are multi-dimensional beings living in a multi-dimensional universe. I describe the ET events which dramatically altered my reality and how these events promoted a more powerful and happier version of myself.

There are parts in the book which may seem scary. They were scary to me, at the time. I now have a different perspective and have transcended the debilitating hold fear had on me. In other words, this is a happy alien story.

So, here I am being the most vulnerable I have ever been. I risk ridicule and that has been a fear I have had my entire life. In order for me to be my most authentic self, I need to face this fear and tell my truth. Here it is. Here is my life-long story about me and the aliens.

THE GREAT AWAKENING
from Randi's book,
4th Dimensional Healing: A Guidebook
For A New Paradigm of Healing

What if we are walking around thinking we are wide awake, but we are actually sleep-walking?

A great shift is taking place on our planet. The earth's energy is rising in vibration. We are all feeling it at some level, from the subtlest sense of a general discomfort with how life has been all this time, to the most astonishing emergence of new psychic and paranormal gifts.

Our world is shifting from the third dimensional reality into the fourth. Each dimension is a different vibrational state that perpetuates certain perceptions and attitudes. In the third dimensional reality we have been living in a purposeful state of perceived separation from everything around us, including Source. This reality creates experiences of polarities: right and wrong, better and worse, light and dark. And as we, as spiritual beings, have perceived ourselves as separate, forgetting ourselves to be the divine expressions of Source Creator, we have struggled to understand our powers and freedoms. The questions that were to be answered were: "What would I do if I could do anything? Who would I be if I could be anyone?"

The acceptance of this belief system has created the world as we know it. If we can look at it without judgment, we can see that in our Free Will universe, we are all at different levels of development. At the most basic level, in third-dimensional reality we feel powerless and we believe that we are victims of what is happening in the world. We believe that everything happens *to* us.

If you told a third-dimensional reality-based person that angels are helping you heal, if they could not see angels, they might not be able to believe it. In third dimensional reality, God is a reflection of a judgmental world. Life is about reward and punishment, and everyone and everything around us is a reflection of that. In the third dimension we believe only what we see - and what we see looks separate and distinct.

The vibration of the fourth dimension brings with it an expansion of awareness that begins to include the ideas that there is a connection between the Self and everything outside of the self and that life is a co-creative experience. Life is about cause and effect, and each one of us is responsible for his own experiences. Within that, each experience is part of a whole, with all facets originating from the vibration of Love, so on an energetic level, no experience is better or worse than any other – although physically, some experiences can seem bad or painful.

At this point, there is a gradual awakening to the idea that there is more to this world than meets the eye (and ear). The concepts of God and other spiritual beings expand as well. God is no longer presumed to be about reward and punishment. Instead, God is an essence, a life-force energy, found in and of everything. Because of this awareness, the heart chakra begins to expand and people feel more unconditionally loved and protected.

In fourth dimensional awareness, people begin to have spiritual experiences that include insights and information from other beings. Intuition develops more fully, stimulating expansions of the five senses to perceive what is not on the physical plane, increasing empathy, precognition, dreams and healing abilities. Connections are made with angelic beings, elementals and alien races.

The fifth dimension will bring an even higher vibration, opening the door to unconditional love and acceptance. People will surrender completely to the Source Creator, with the understanding that self and God are not separate, but part of the same whole. Nonjudgment, unity, community and mastery are the perceptions of the fifth dimension.

This movement from one perspective to another, higher vibrational perspective, can be seen beginning to emerge in the 1960s, as many people began to question norms with the resulting social, civic and political dissonance. The transition gained momentum in the 1970s with the self-help movement and has continued into the present. During the 1970s people felt allowed to begin "searching for themselves" in ways they were never allowed to do before. During that decade we witnessed a rise in personal transformation practices such as self awareness, self improvement, yoga, meditation, tai chi, alternative healing, natural foods, etc. There was a general call to understand more about the self and each other, and tap into a broader reality. Divorce was on the rise, as people began searching for, and feeling that they had a right to, a greater sense of fulfillment from life. Life became less about survival (3rd dimension) and more about connection (4th dimension).

Another way to describe this transformative time is to say that it was the beginning of the transition from the Piscean Age into the Aquarian Age. Each astrological age is based on the tilt of the Earth as it spins on its axis. Each age lasts approximately 2,160 years (some resources differ on the exact number of years). Each is linked to one of the twelve astrological signs, with a full cycle beginning again every 25,920 years. Additionally, each age is linked to major cultural, societal and political changes on the planet.

For the last 2100 years we were living in the Piscean Age, a time that governed the belief in hierarchical powers that lie outside of ourselves. People lived by the tenet that it was important to find someone or something externally to believe in. The Piscean Age was associated with research about the truth hidden behind what is perceived by the five senses, which corresponds to the mysteries associated with Christ's life. It was also the time during which the truth of our essential duality—body (form) and soul—was revealed. The evolutionary work of this Age has been the lifting of our lower physical nature to that of the soul.

The shift from the Piscean to the Aquarian Age occurred over the last fifty years. Some say the Aquarian Age began on November 11, 2011 and others say began on December 12, 2012. This new age carries with it the energy of looking within ourselves to find our power. There is an expectation that the Aquarian age will usher in a period of group consciousness. As the water-bearer, Aquarius may signify that humans will be less egoistic and more in the mindset of service to others rather than service to self. We will see a rise in widespread transparent, peaceful, neighborly, and sustainable living. Humanity will evolve to understand more of its place among the stars and think more in a universal manner.

This time period we live in now has been called an awakening, or an ascension. The entire planet is shifting into this new vibration, this new consciousness. It has allowed us to experience heightened senses of awareness on every level — physical, mental, emotional and spiritual. Human beings are feeling the urge to understand themselves better, create more positive relationships and find community. In contrast, while many positive personal changes have emerged, we have also seen an increase in maladies such as depression, suicide, anxiety, stress, and alcohol and drug abuse (both pharmaceutical and recreational).

As more people suffer in these ways, they look for options for relieving their pain. More and more people are eschewing the kind of impersonal, rote western medical model that has dominated for the last one hundred years. There is a call to attend to the deeper levels of the individual with more "natural" and holistic methods of addressing the body's dysfunctions. There is a greater understanding of the fact that we are energetic beings and we can access that energy through all sorts of techniques being taught to the layperson these days: various forms of Reiki, Psych-K, Theta Healing, Emotional Freedom Technique (EFT), Access Consciousness and so many more.

Millions are waking up now; ready to heal themselves and desiring to heal others. Lightworkers everywhere are working towards "cleaning up" the impact of our fear-based beliefs in order to help life on this planet thrive — thereby creating Heaven on Earth.

The Fourth Dimensional Healer

In the past, our notions about "healing" have been focused on fixing what was wrong. Illness was seen as the absence of wellness. The commonly held belief was that we were the victims of illness, and being sick was just bad luck. Disease was seen as being caused by some invader from the outside world (bacteria, viruses, cancers) or because of some biochemical imbalance (for example, an allergy is too much histamine and depression is not enough serotonin). The goal of treatment was to kill the invader or chemically "adjust" the biochemistry.

The fourth dimensional healing model begs us to consider that physical issues are manifestations of negative emotions and thoughts that form the foundation of our perceptions. Additionally, our perceptions create our realities, therefore negative thoughts and emotions (all of which stem from fear-based beliefs) create negative experiences in our lives.

However, does being a healer mean you have to assume something is wrong or that something needs to be fixed?

Assuming something needs to be fixed is a judgment. Judgment comes from a third-dimensional perspective. To presume that we can judge anyone (including ourselves) or anything assumes that we have access to the entirety of information that there is. It presumes that we know what each and every person's soul experience is *supposed* to be, and beyond that, that there are *right* and *wrong* ways of being. The fact that we have been pressured into believing in right and wrong, or better and worse, has been deemed by many spiritual teachers as being the actual definition of "original sin."

I think this (anonymous) quote says it perfectly:

"Thinking you know what other people need is the ultimate arrogance. Allow people the dignity of their own struggle."

Or, another way to put it might be"

"Who am I to interfere with your suffering?"

To approach healing from a place of negativity creates more negativity. Really think about it: negativity is a result of fear, so the energy that we are holding in our bodies as we work on our client is a vibration of fear. So the whole session is somewhat (and probably completely unintentionally) couched in fear, which sets the stage for, not necessarily more fear, but surely a lack of pure Light (love). Instead, we must enter the session knowing that we are all spiritual beings of God, having experiences that ultimately contribute to soul growth.

As we transition into the fourth dimension we understand that this planet of free will allows for an infinite number of possibilities for every situation and every decision. Therefore, no one gets to impose right or wrong on anyone else. How each of us looks, thinks, acts, dresses, smells, worships and moves through life is *supposed* to be individual and unique.

Everyone alive on the planet at this time has committed to remembering themselves as aspects of Divinity, whether or not they happen to be aware of this fact. We are each choosing to do that in different ways. We each have taken different soul paths and so will have different needs during this transformation. Your job as a healer, or when healing yourself, is to hold space for anything that shows up, while supporting others as they remember their innate connection to Source.

Healing happens in layers. The layers run through all the different lifetimes, soul paths, emotional issues and soul challenges. They run through the Divine Identity, Divine Function and Divine Essence of each being, which make up the core parts of each person's personality. The layers of healing run through the five energetic bodies (or *koshas*), as well as the three energy bodies: the mental, emotional and spiritual bodies. (See the chapter on *Energy Bodies*.) The great thing about fourth dimensional energetic healing is that you as the healer don't need to have any of that information. The spiritual healing team holds that knowledge and the angelic healers do the work that needs to be done. Read the chapter on the spiritual healing team to learn who is present for each person.

ONE DEFINITION
A Channeled Message by Sev

Each of you are your own microcosms living in unison with billions of realities.

We would like to play a game with you today. We ask you to pretend you are a visitor to Earth from another reality which houses living beings and natural beauty. We ask you to take the view of a foreigner to your realm. In this game, we wish to guide you towards self-empowerment.

Upon the acceptance of a detached view, will you be able to see the simplicity of your Earth. Yes, it's simple in its workings. Through various civilizations and control seekers, you are under the belief that your planet is complex. The only complexity is that which rules your minds into believing you are operating in a gigantic sea of turmoil and frustration.

Do you realize how much power results from detachment? Your freedom is directly proportional to your mental attachments. An attachment is that which represents you. An attachment is that which you have determined to be your adjective. How many adjectives have you accumulated in hopes of projecting an image of yourself which is only a delusion to keep you from yourself?

Are you attached to being fair? Are you attached to being hard-working? Are you attached to wearing expensive items? For every adjective - fair, hard-working, rich, kind, smart, polite, caring, etc - you take one step further from yourself in hopes of clouding over what you really are. Your true nature is neutral - neither kind nor mean, neither smart nor dumb. Do you know which energy is the most neutral of all? Love.

Can you consider having only one adjective? The one being loving? From there, don't define yourself. Because, sometimes you kind ones are not kind. And you honest ones are not honest. And when you act out of your self-imposed definitions, you feel guilt and blame is then allowed to enter. If you never labeled yourself as polite, when you are rude, you will not give yourself a guilt trip. And if you label your-self a SOB, you will not think you are losing your powerful edge when you are kind.

Your self-imposed definitions is your recipe for get-ting what you want. Recipes grow outdated. And recipes also deter experimentation. If you substitute and play around with the ingredients, you produce a completely different re-sult. So, we ask you, *What's in your recipe?* What are the in-gredients (adjectives) working together to produce the dish called "*you*?"

How comfortable are you in eliminating some or all the ingredients except for the one which must exist or noth-ing exists, which is love?

Imagine the freedom of only being love. So, this allows you to act as your heart desires in any given second in any given situation. Imagine living so you don't have to sustain and support your recipe of being. When you declare, *"I am love and that's it,"* you can be an SOB when you want and Mother Teresa in the next second. And you will finally feel the freedom you innately search for. This is the true nature of yourselves - free. You are not bound to cosmic contracts or karma. You are bound to nothing. You were not forced to experience the Earth consciousness. It is a field trip you signed up for.

As the Alien visitor we ask you to pretend to be, what do you see on this planet? Harmony. Yes. Discord. Yes. Love. Yes. Hate. Yes. Nurture. Yes. Torture. Yes. How schizophrenic your Earth is. And for those of you who exhibit this, you are labeled disturbed and sick. Yet, each and every one of you house the same energy. Some of you have chosen to exhibit one side of it more than the other - the kind more than the rude or the lazy more than the hard-working. Some of you wish to explore more gradients of your dual energies. But your society wants you to define yourself and stick to that definition - otherwise you are troubled or mental or sick or going through "something" like a mid-life crisis. There is no permission to change on your Earth. You better stick to your definitions, or you are having a life problem, a mental breakdown.

So, you, the Alien, are witnessing the cosmic dance of self-identity. And it is comical because it is a behavior which is self-defeating and self-imposed and the waves of energy created from your inability to freely expose your mind causes the same disaster over and over. If you watched the Titanic hit the iceberg over and over, you would laugh in disbelief. The first disaster wasn't enough? It had to go back for another? Many of you live your lives like that. And the reason is because you refuse to let go of your definitions.

The Alien sees every human encompassing every adjective existing on your realm. For all ways of being and their correlated energies rest in your Earth planet aura, also known as Earth's Collective Consciousness. So, to the Alien each one of you are everything on Earth. Each of you are all of Earth. Each of you are ugly and beautiful, murderous and life-supporting, patient and impatient. And in any second, any adjective can be expressed. Will you allow the expression of any emotion? For when you give yourself the freedom, only then will you have it. No one gives you freedom but yourself. You are the cop, the judge, the jailer, the warden, and the executioner. These energies rest in all of you.

Where is your focus, all you mighty judges? Where do your thoughts like to linger? In how you think someone else did something wrong? It's comical to the Alien how consumed you are with other people's actions and the efforts made to hold others to their definitions. The Alien wonders why you don't turn that microscope gaze upon yourself. If you looked at yourself under the hyper-powerful, mega-super, cosmic microscope, there would be just one element visible - love.

The Alien wonders why the humans ignore their one, basic building block. If you didn't ignore the love within you, you would be in love with yourself. And if you were in love with yourself, you'd be what ever you are in that moment. The freedom to be and the freedom to express are bringers of joy to your hearts.

The next time someone asks you to describe yourself in 3 words, may you consider, *"I am love, loving, and loved."*

The love that runs through you is the same love running through us. We love you for we know no other way to be...thank you.

THE AQUARIAN AGE
A Channeled Message by Randi

Following is a message I received from The Council of Federations as a response to my questions about channeling spirits. The Federation members were quick to inform me that they are here, within closer reach than ever before. They, along with many, many other spirits, guides, masters and teachers, are waiting for us to form relationships with them.

Your mind is not the only aspect of you. Your mind operates in questions: "What if?" "How can I?" "What next?" "Why?" Your Divine Self, the part that lives within, through and around you, knows only flow. It follows a predestined course, like a river that carries you through life. How you respond to the events and experiences along the way is up to you.

Those who relate to themselves as a mind in a body (and only as that), keep from acknowledging greater connections and opportunities to the universe beyond. How can one do or create something one has no belief in? Each of you only conceive what you believe.

As a natural and innate occurrence, people move in and out of deeper self-connection all day. The Divine Self moves the river along, guiding happenstance and events.

And no matter what choices are made or what reactions are had, you never leave the river or get lost.

The Divine Self is the soul aspect of each person and that soul lives in the higher dimensions of existence. Within those dimensions, the soul operates in conjunction with other spirit beings — guides, masters and teachers. As mentioned above, your life is like a river, and we (the spirit members of the Federation) walk alongside, occasionally reaching in to assist, clear your path, or drop in a life raft.

Your free will allows you to accept or not accept help at any time.

Your ability to quiet your thoughts allows you to reach into our connect to you — and your connection to us. Take time to breathe. Take time to quiet. Find the safe place within you where you can go to be still and slow and connected to your heart.

We are closer than ever before, easier access, due to vibrational changes happening to you and the planet. Every person has the ability to connect and will do so somewhat differently. This may be easiest via automatic writing; meditating; looking for signs; lyrics in songs, etc.

We will find our ways to communicate with you. We will learn each other's languages. Our desire is strong as we feel a stronger urging to do this work with you because we are bound by vows to assist in this planetary ascension. This is an exciting and exhilarating time for us! We use this opportunity to work off our own karma, contribute to the benefit of the Universe and thus achieve our own ascension as we reach you.

There are millions of spirits eager to connect, waiting for their turn to assist and serve. And as more people reach out to and trust the benevolent factors in the Universe, the more Light-infused your planet becomes.

In the Aquarian Age, the 5th-dimensional earth, hearts and minds will open, understanding will flourish. There will be compassion and Love for All , not only for all people, but for all aspects of all people. Misdeeds will be seen and known for what they are: fear-based and pain-filled actions and reactions. This knowledge will give way to forgiveness. There will be opportunity for great healing.

NOTES

NOTES

NOTES

Made in the USA
Middletown, DE
20 November 2020

24570056R00033